Prancer
the
DEMON
Chihuahua

Jokes, Activities, and More!

Pam Pho
Illustrated by Cloris Chou

Andrews McMeel
PUBLISHING®

Andrews McMeel Publishing
a division of Andrews McMeel Universal
1130 Walnut Street, Kansas City, Missouri 64106

www.andrewsmcmeel.com

22 23 24 25 26 27 28 SDB 10 9 8 7 6 5 4 3 2 1

ISBN: 978-1-5248-7612-8

Library of Congress Control Number: 2022940178

Editor: Erinn Pascal
Art Director/Designer: Julie Barnes
Production Editor: Jennifer Straub
Production Manager: Chuck Harper

Made by:
RR Donnelley (Guangdong) Printing Solutions Co., Ltd.
Address and location of production:
Daning Administrative District, Humen Town
Dongguan Guangdong, China 523930
1st Printing — 9/26/22

ATTENTION: SCHOOLS AND BUSINESSES
Andrews McMeel books are available at quantity discounts
with bulk purchase for educational, business, or sales
promotional use. For information, please e-mail the
Andrews McMeel Publishing Special Sales Department:
sales@amuniversal.com.

Wanted: Home for Chihuahua

Written By: Tyfanee, Chihuahua's Foster Mom

OK, I've tried. For the last several months I've attempted to post Prancer for adoption and make him sound like a good dog. You know what I'm talking about. The kind of dog that will curl on your lap and offer you kisses or, at the very least, the kind of dog that will lounge on the couch and let you do your own thing. A nice, happy, tail-wagging dog.

The problem is ... Prancer is *not* a good dog.

Every day, I live in the grips of this demonic Chihuahua. He pees. He bites. He barks at everything. He's 50 percent hate and 50 percent tremble.

But I must believe there's someone out there for Prancer, because I am tired and so is my family.

Hi, I'm Prancer. I'm low-key famous on the internet because of the ad my foster mom wrote about me. She said I was "demonic." The truth is I was kind of a bad dog. OK, I'll be real, I was a <u>VERY BAD</u> dog. Then, I met my new owner-slash-victim, Ariel. She likes bacon, egg, and cheese sandwiches. I like to steal bacon, egg, and cheese sandwiches. She doesn't care too much for neighbors; I hate most people. I like to model; she likes to take photos of me.

Ariel and I have a lot in common but that doesn't mean this is going to work out.

We'll see if she still wants to hang out after I pee in her favorite backpack.

Let's talk about
all of the things
I **don't** like.

Cats.

Have you ever met a cat that wasn't plotting to take over the world? Yeah. Me neither.

Ten reasons why cats are the worst:

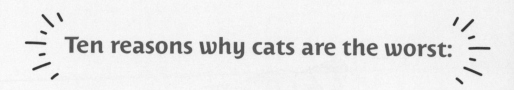

1. They are not dogs

2. The hissing

3. The claws

4. The cattitude

5. They're bigger than me
   and I don't like it

6. They poop in a box inside of your house

7. They don't go for walks

8. Cats are bullies

9. I'm allergic

10. They are cats

Other things I don't like:

BARK! BARK!

Most people, but *ESPECIALLY* this guy ...

No thanks to **vegetables**. If it isn't beef
or bacon, egg, and cheese sandwiches,
I don't want it.

Squirrels.

I don't think they need an introduction.

They are BAD NEWS.

Birds, and basically all small animals.
Maybe I love them instead of hate them …
they're just super fun to chase.

I wonder what
would happen
if I caught a **bird**
or a **squirrel**....

Mops. They are evil and must be destroyed at all costs. There is no greater enemy. (Except maybe the squirrels.)

This list is getting long. Let's talk about some of the things I **love**.

I love **clothes**.

I also love **modeling** my clothes.

Food. Food is great. Here are my five favorite top foods.

1. Bacon

2. Eggs

3. Cheese

4. Sandwiches

5. Bacon, egg, and cheese sandwiches

An Ode to Bacon, Egg, and Cheese Sandwiches
a poem by Prancer

If I were a sandwich, I would be a bacon,
egg, and cheese sandwich
Would thou eat me
With cheddar cheese?

Verily, I would eat thee
If thou wert a bacon and egg sandwich
Indeed, I would

Dreaming of eggy cheesy beef
Drooling on my pillow
Until we meet again

I love movies! Sit on the couch with a snack and relax. Here are my top ten movies:

1. 101 Chihuahuas (way better than the original)

2. The Fast and the Furriest

3. Prancer and the Squirrel

4. All Dogs Go to the Coffee Shop

5. Air Prancer

6. Pet Store Bound

7. Prancer: A Dog's Tale

8. Isle of Prancers

9. Lady and the Prancer

10. Hotel for Prancer

The jury is still out on if
I love my new **victim**, Ariel.

Victim used to stay home a lot. Now she has me. **We go** a lot of places.

Ma'am, do you have a permit to conceal carry that chihuahua?

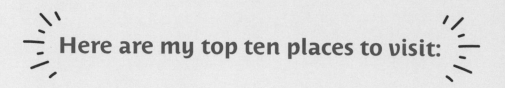

Here are my top ten places to visit:

1. **Fast Food**
   Bacon, egg, and cheese sandwiches. Enough said.

2. **The Beach**
   But don't put a bikini on me.

3. **The Park**
   President of the Anti-Squirrel Association over here!

4. **My Grandpawrents' House**
   Just remember, they're *my* grandpawrents, not yours.

5. **New York City**
   Bacon, egg, and cheese city!

6. The Photo Studio

I get lots of attention. I like attention.

7. Pet Store

I get lots of toys. I like toys.

8. Coffee Shop

Both attention AND toys. Victim calls them straws. I call them toys.

9. Restaurants

Especially if they have bacon, egg, and cheese sandwiches.

10. Obedience Class

But not always.

Funny story about going to the coffee shop incoming!

So, Victim and I were at the Bucks (that's what we call it because we are cool like that) drive-through. Apparently, I'm not allowed inside. Which is absurd, because I bet I'm better behaved than a baby, and they can go inside. . . .

Anyway, at the window, they forgot my Puppuccino. Ariel asked for it again but the lady at the window couldn't stop staring at me in the car.

Finally, the lady smiled big and said, "Oh my gosh, is that Prancer!?"

That was the entire story. I just wanted to remind you that I'm famous now. And don't furr-get it.

I've come up with some **good jokes** lately. Wanna hear them? Of course you do. I'm telling them.

There are no aggressive breeds of dog.

10. Aggression

9. Is

8. Not

7. Bred

6. It

5. Is

4. A

3. Trained

2. Behavior

1. Chihuahua

GRRR...

Chihuahuas are
a lot like farts.
Only their ~~victims~~
owners can
stand them.

Who is Santa's favorite reindeer?

Prancer.

(Obviously.)

If a tree falls in a forest,
a Chihuahua 500 miles away
will start barking.

"Don't bite the hand
that feeds you.
Bite their ankles instead!"

– a Chihuahua

What is a Chihuahua's favorite book?

Green Eggs and Ham (Sandwiches!)

What is a Chihuahua's favorite TV show?

Sesame Str—er, Bagel!

**What do you call
a Chihuahua in the snow?**

Slush puppy.

**What do you call
a Chihuahua in the rain?**

Mad.

Why do Chihuahuas like going camping?

Because they get to *ruff* it!

OK, enough jokes. I have another funny story for you.

I was at the spa—er, ~~Victim's~~ Ariel's bathroom—when I unleashed the MOST silent-but-deadly fart ... ever.

I thought I was in the clear and no one noticed. The water started bubbling like a volcano erupting and Ariel looked at me.

I glared back at her.

Go ahead. Accuse me. Say something, I dared her. Because this is really her fault.

She shouldn't have left her bean burrito unattended earlier.

Time for a quiz break.

How Prancer are you? Circle your answer below to find out!

1. **Do you like cheese?**
   a. Yes
   b. No

2. **Do you like peeing in random places?**
   a. Yes
   b. No

3. **Do you like to chase squirrels?**
   a. Yes
   b. No

4. **Do you like modeling new clothes?**
   a. Yes
   b. No

5. **Do you hate the mail carriers?**
   a. Yes
   b. No

Now count how many a's you circled to find your answer!

1–2 a's

You're not like Prancer at all. Live a little. Eat the cheesy, eggy, sandwichey goodness.

2–3 a's

You're getting there but you need to work on your squirrel chasing skills.

4–5 a's

You have unleashed your inner demonic Chihuahua and are an expert at sabotaging all mail carriers. Congrats!

STORYTIME!

One day, Ariel took me for a drive. We pulled up at a cozy house and I saw someone standing on the porch. I looked at Ariel because she *knows* I don't like new people.

I got out of the car only because there are trees, and trees mean squirrels, and squirrels mean chasing.

There's a lady there, too. She bends down and bows. *Well, that's proper respect, I think,* and go over to her. She hands me a bacon, egg, and cheese sandwich.

Ariel tells me this is my grandma. I've decided that grandmas are great.

So, bonus point for you. If you like grandmas, you're even more Prancer than we thought.

I have my own social media accounts.
Sometimes my fans make memes
of my photos.

When you're **short** and
you hit that five-foot
section of the pool.

When someone tries to take my food.

When I'm trying to take someone's food.

Roses are red ... I'm going to **bed**.

When you show someone
a **meme** and they say
they've already seen it.

Sometimes Ariel goes to work
and I'm left alone.

When she's gone, I like to nap.
There are lots of places to nap, like...

The sofa...

…And **under the bed**.

I also like to **dance**.

If I get **bored**, I pee on things I shouldn't.

An Ode to Peeing
on Things I Shouldn't

a poem by Prancer

If you leave it on the floor, I will pee on it
Would thou be angry?
Tis thine own fault

Verily, I would pee on this
If thee leave it on a floor
Indeed, I would

Backpacks, purses, socks, and shoes
I lift my leg and mark them as mine
Until thou learnst to pick thine items up

**To keep Ariel on her toes,
I choose different places to hide
my revenge pees.**

1. Her closet by the shoes
   (sometimes in a shoe)

2. Under the dining room table

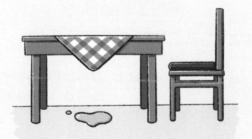

3. Under the bed

4. Right beside the door (this means *MAYBE* she'll step in it when she comes home)

5. If I'm super mad and she's gone all day, I'll pee on the couch or her bed

When Ariel is at home writing,
I like to listen to her playlists.

From Ariel's playlists I've found my top ten favorite songs. I hope when you listen to them you think of me eating a bacon, egg, and cheese sandwich.

1. Push It – Salt-N-Puppa

2. Love Yourself – Justin Beagle

3. Basenji Rhapsody – Queensland Heeler

4. Hey Yorkie! – OutKat

5. Someone Like You – Akita

6. Seamus – Poodle Floyd

7. Barky – Fur-rell Williams

8. Once Bitten Twice Shy – Great Pyrenees

9. Break Free from My Leash – Ari-yawn-a Grande

10. Gimme a Bone – George Thorogood-boy

If I use my fame to become a pop star, I'm going to name myself Prancer *Venti* so that I'm **bigger** than Ari-yawn-a *Grande*. (That's a Puppaccino joke!)

Ariel and I have adapted to living together.
We have some **chill parties**.

We take lots of **trips**.

There's **a lot to do** on a trip.
You never know what you're
going to see.

One time, in New York, I got to see a lot of art. I decided to become **an artist**. Here's some of the best paintings I can imagine.

The Statue of Liber-TINY

The Scream

By: Anyone Who Meets a Chihuahua, Probably

Mona Prancer

But this is my **favorite** piece of art.

If you **don't** like my art, this is what I have to say to you:

Learn how to speak Prancer!

Boof – A timid small
sound I make
to test reactions.

Woof – When I am excited.
These are mainly saved
for squirrels and sandwiches.

Bark - It's about to go down.
What is going down?
I don't know. But something.

Here are some facts about Chihuahuas:

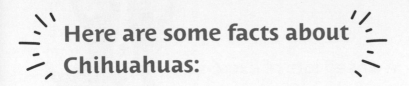

1. We love our family very much and probably have a favorite person.

2. We don't really like strangers or new situations.

3. We don't like to be separated from our family.

4. We are super happy and excited, but we need really good training so we don't mistake excited for angry.

5. We are heckin' boofers and boofers gonna boof.

6. We need lots of exercise and stimulation.

7. We get super old. Like 18 years old! (That's 126 in human years!)

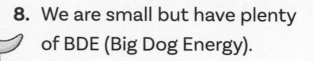

8. We are small but have plenty of BDE (Big Dog Energy).

9. We originated from the Techichi, which was another breed of dog in Mexico.

10. We are 100 percent the best dogs ever.

Chihuahuas are considered **companion** dogs. I take guarding my family very seriously.

I realize I called Ariel "victim" at first. Now, she's Ariel. But I think she may be becoming my **family**. I would probably guard her from something. I need to think about this more....

Before I came into her life, Ariel says she was kind of like a hermit. Now, she must take me on vacations and has found a lot of friends on the internet.

Plus, I need a lot of **walkies**. It's either that or I pee on her sofa again.

Ariel has a lot to do now. There's my laundry, my snacks, my meals, her training, my meals, fashion shows.... The list is **never-ending**.

It gets **super cold** where we live in Connecticut in the winter. I've tried to convince Ariel to move to Florida, but I've failed.

This means I'm **stuck** wearing winter coats and boots.

I am **no fan** of the boots.

Every day is a little different, but I think I have it down to a science. My schedule is...

A Day in the Life of Prancer

6:00–7:00 a.m. – Pretend I don't hear Ariel trying to get me up to go for a walk so that she can go to work. (If I don't get up, she can't go to work.)

7:00–7:30 a.m. – Sniff everything and hold my potty for as long as I can to make Ariel late for work.

7:30–7:31 a.m. – Scarf down breakfast and ask for seconds.

7:31–7:40 a.m. – Eat second breakfast. (I take longer with this one so Ariel will be even later for work.)

7:40–8:00 a.m. – Bark relentlessly until I get a treat.

8:00 a.m.–5:30 p.m. – Nap and be mad that Ariel is gone. Maybe pee in her backpack, if I'm feeling festive.

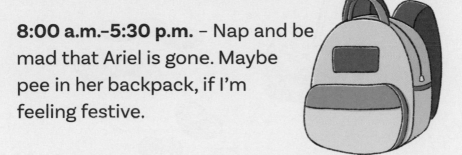

5:30–5:45 p.m. – Refuse to go on walkies until I am given cheese.

5:45–6:30 p.m. – Big walkies. Gotta get my step count in for the day.

6:30–9:00 p.m. – Dinner and a movie with Ariel before bed.

One of my favorite holidays is **Halloween**.
There's candy! I also love getting dressed up.
This year, I had several costumes.

An Adorable Lion

Why are **dragons** good storytellers?

Because they all have **tales**!

Don't ask about this one.

Autumn is **great** in general because it's not too hot or too cold. It's the perfect weather for sweaters!

The seasons listed by my preferences:

1. Fall

2. Spring

3. Summer

4. (replace 4 with 100) Winter

Besides the fact it's too cold and I must wear boots, there are **NO SQUIRRELS** to chase in winter.

The birds are few and far between as well. There are **cats**, but they aren't even fun to chase.

Honestly, I have no idea what Ariel
would do without me.

OK.

I have an idea.

I think I'm going to start calling her
"Mom."

It's been a year and we
are a **family** now.

Now that we're a family,
I have many, many plans. There are
breakfasts to be stolen, mail carriers
to sabotage, and new things Mom got
for the holidays to be **peed on**.

BARK!
BARK!

So long as Mom can deal with me
being a fashionista, icon, and heckin'
good **boofer**!

I want to thank **Second Chance Pet Rescue** for finding my new mom and taking care of me when I didn't have a home. I'd also like to thank cheese, squirrels, bacon, and cheeseburgers.

I want to thank Tyfanee Fortuna, Prancer's foster mom, for choosing me to adopt him. A huge thank you to Last Chance Adoption for helping animals like Prancer find homes. Most importantly, I'd like to thank Prancer. He has challenged me every day to be the best version of myself and I don't know what I'd do without him.

Ariel

I want to thank Prancer for bringing so much light into the world during a pandemic. I'd also like to thank Ariel, his mom, for trusting me to write this book and help spread the love of Prancer even farther. I haven't met a more patient and kind editor than Erinn Pascal. She guided Ariel, Prancer, and I through this process and made this book so much more fun. I'd like to thank the team at Andrews McMeel for taking care of us and being so involved in this process. Cloris, your illustrations made everything so much brighter. You are a true artist. I'd like to thank my mom and my step-dad for letting me read constantly. To my husband Brandon and my children Addie and Elijah, thank you for reading this during every revision and helping me make better jokes. To Dolly Parton for starting the Imagination Library. A very special thank you to my elementary school librarian Ms. White, you gave a young farm girl the gift of reading and that lasted a lifetime.

Pam